my first book of
QUESTIONS AND ANSWERS
about
LONG
LONG AGO

Maggie Brown

p

This is a Parragon Book
First published in 2001

Parragon
Queen Street House
4 Queen Street
Bath BA1 1HE, UK

Copyright © Parragon 2001

Produced by

David West Children's Books
7 Princeton Court
55 Felsham Road
Putney
London SW15 1AZ

British Library Cataloguing-in-Publication Data

A catalogue record for this book is available from the British Library.

ISBN 0-75255-845-5

Printed in China

Designers
Aarti Parmar, Rob Shone, Fiona Thorne

Illustrators
Chris Brown, Steve Caldwell, Mark Dolby,
Gerry Haylock, Graham Kennedy,
Andy Lloyd Jones, Pete Roberts
(Allied Artists)
James Field (SGA)

Cartoonist
Peter Wilks (SGA)

Editor
James Pickering

CONTENTS

WHY WERE MAMMOTHS WOOLLY? and other questions about prehistoric animals

26 Which was the tallest bird?

27 What were the first whales like?

28 What were sabre-toothed cats like?

28 Which animals attacked sabre-tooths?

29 How big were the first bears?

30 Which was the biggest-ever land mammal?

30 Which was the ugliest mammal?

31 Which deer had branch-sized antlers?

32 When were horses the size of foxes?

33 When were elephants the size of pigs?

34 Why were mammoths woolly?

35 Why did mammoths die out?

WHICH DINOSAUR WAS A BIGHEAD? and other questions about dinosaurs

38 How big were the biggest dinosaurs?

39 How small were the smallest dinosaurs?

40 How many kinds of dinosaur were there?

41 When did dinosaurs live?

41 What sort of animal were they?

42 How do we know about dinosaurs?

42 How were fossils made?

43 What kind of dinosaur fossils do scientists find?

44 What did dinosaurs eat?

45 Why do scientists love dinosaur droppings?

45 Did dinosaurs eat grass?

46 Who was king of the dinosaurs?

47 What colour was Tyrannosaurus?

47 Who was the giant dinosaur?

48 Which dinosaur went fishing?

49 Which dinosaur had a sail on its back?

49 Who was the biggest fish-eater?

50 Which dinosaur had a long big toenail?

51 Are model dinosaurs true to life?

52 Which dinosaurs cracked a whip?

53 Were long-necked dinosaurs brainy?

53 Why did the long-necked dinosaurs eat stones?

54 Which dinosaurs had duckbills?

55 Who liked to blow his own trumpet?

55 Who was the helmet lizard?

56 Were dinosaurs good parents?

56 Which dinosaur laid the biggest egg?

57 Which of the dinosaurs was an egg robber?

58 Why did Triceratops have horns?

59 Who were headbangers?

59 Which dinosaur was a bighead?

60 Why were some dinosaurs built like tanks?

61 Which dinosaur spiked its enemies?

61 Which dinosaur packed a mean punch?

62 How fast could dinosaurs run?

63 What were dinobirds?

64 What happened to the dinosaurs?

65 Are any dinosaurs alive today?

WHO WERE THE FIRST PEOPLE?
and other questions about early people

68 Who were the first people?

69 Who was Lucy?

70 What was the Stone Age?

70 What were early tools used for?

71 When were weapons invented?

72 Why were Stone Age people great travellers?

73 Who were the first Americans?

74 Which bright sparks lit the first fires?

74 Why was fire useful?

75 How did Stone Age people light fires?

76 Who were the Neanderthals?

76 Were Neanderthal people stupid?

77 How did Neanderthals hunt with fire?

78 What other animals did people hunt?

79 How did people cook?

79 Did they have cooking pots?

80 Did Stone Age people live in caves?

81 Why did mammoths come in handy?

81 Did Stone Age people build villages?

82 Who were the first artists?

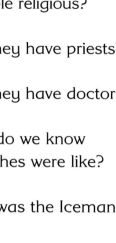

83 What paints did they use?

83 Who were the first musicians?

84 Were Stone Age people religious?

84 Did they have priests?

85 Did they have doctors?

86 How do we know what clothes were like?

87 Who was the Iceman?

88 Did people wear jewellery?

88 Did they carry lucky charms?

89 Did they cut their hair?

90 Who were the first farmers?

91 Did they keep cows?

91 Did they have pets?

92 When were the first towns built?

93 How big were they?

Why were mammoths woolly?

and other questions about prehistoric animals

When did life on Earth begin?

The first-known living things appeared in the oceans about 3,500 million years ago. That's just over 1,000 million years after Earth itself formed.

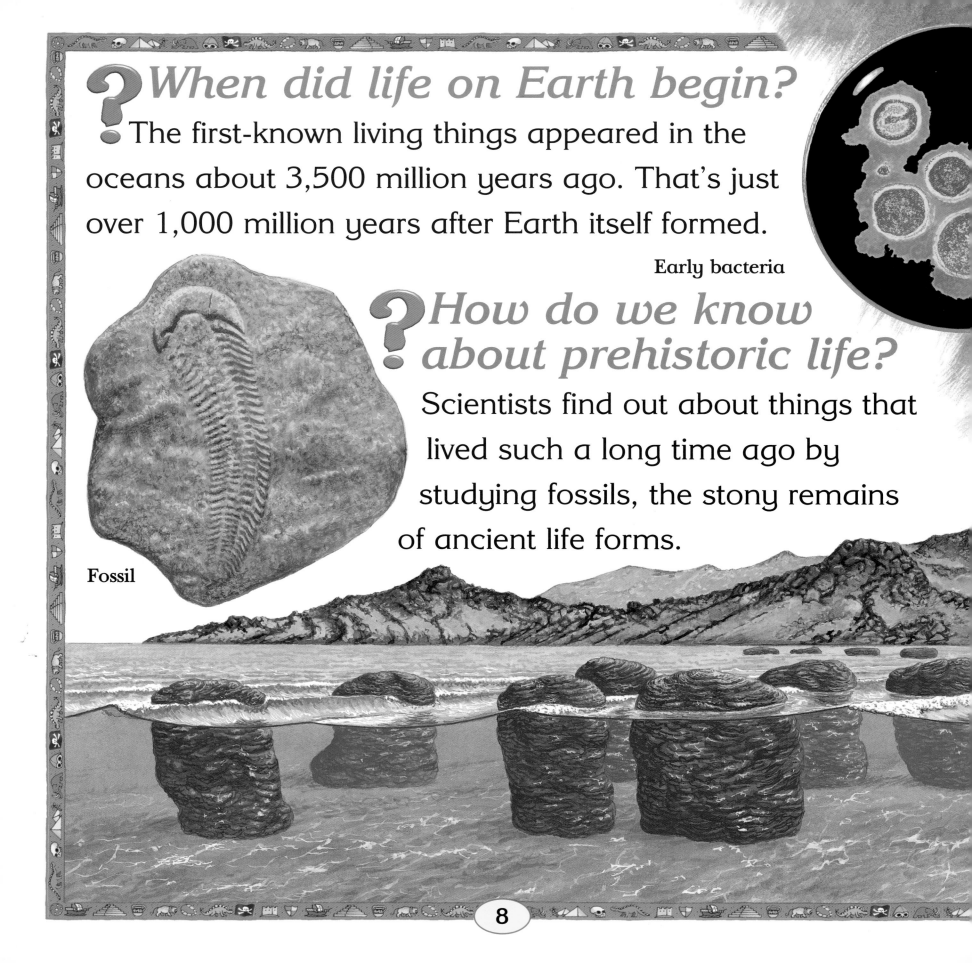

Early bacteria

How do we know about prehistoric life?

Scientists find out about things that lived such a long time ago by studying fossils, the stony remains of ancient life forms.

Fossil

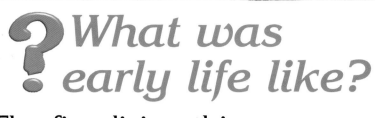
?*What was early life like?*

The first living things were microscopically tiny bacteria. Each one was a single living unit called a cell, and hundreds of them would have fitted on this full stop. Sometimes, layer upon layer of the tiny cells built up in shallow water, creating big mounds that scientists call stromatolites.

Stromatolites

TRUE OR FALSE?

Life might have begun even earlier.

TRUE. It may have started 4,000 million years ago, but scientists haven't found any fossils to prove this.

People used to think Earth formed 6,000 years ago.

TRUE. In 1650, an Irish archbishop said that the Bible showed Earth was created in 4004 BC.

? When did the first bigger creatures appear?

Life on Earth evolved slowly, and the first-known multi-celled sea creatures didn't appear until about 800 million years ago. They had no bones or shells, and they looked a bit like worms and jellyfish.

Soft-bodied creatures on the sea bed 800 million years ago

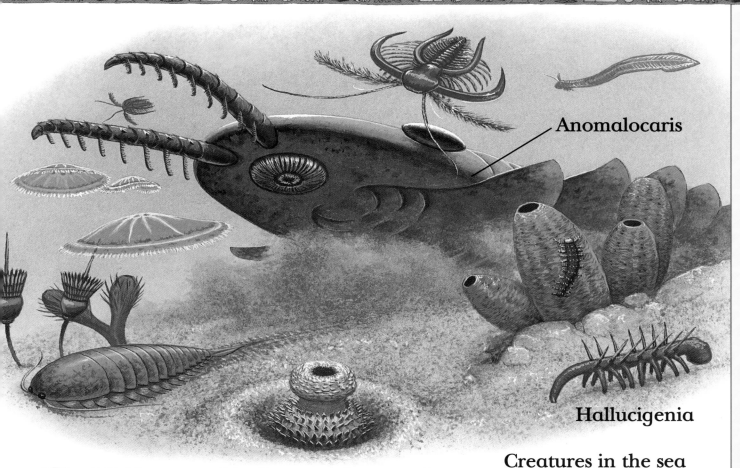

Anomalocaris

Hallucigenia

Creatures in the sea
550 million years ago

❓ *Why did animals grow shells?*

The first-known sea animals with shells began to appear about 550 million years ago. Shells are rather like armour, protecting soft-bodied creatures from attack by enemies. One of the biggest and fiercest of the early animals was Anomalocaris, at about 60 cm long.

Sacabambaspis

Drepanaspis

? *What were the first fish like?*

Fish had appeared in the oceans by 500 million years ago. They were the first animals to have a proper backbone, but they had no fins, and looked a bit like tadpoles. Fish with jaws and teeth came along a few million years later.

? *Which fish was as big as a car?*

Dunkleosteus was a 3.5 m-long killing machine. Its head was protected by armour-like bony plates, while more bony plates lined its jaws. These were razor sharp – all the better to bite you with!

Dunkleosteus

? *Which shark was rough and ready?*

Stethacanthus was a weird early shark with rough, teethlike bristles on top of its head. The top of the T-shaped fin on its back was covered with rough bristles, too.

Stethacanthus

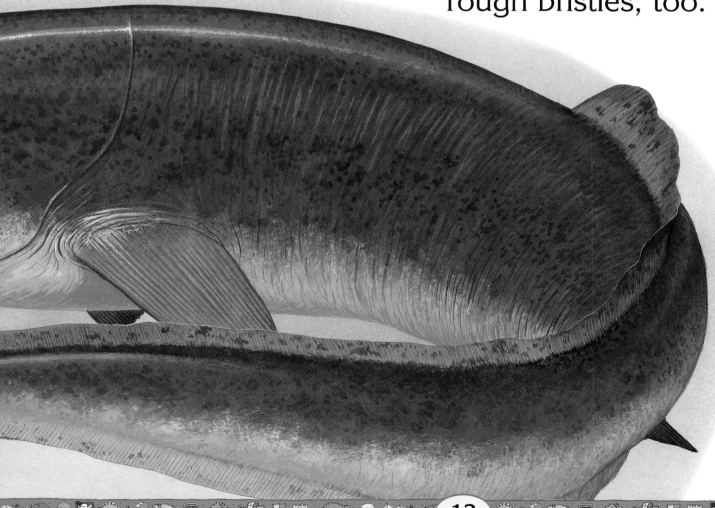

❓Which were the first land animals?

The first-known landlubbers were small spiders, millipedes and insects. By 300 million years ago there were dragonflies the size of kites, and millipedes twice as long as a bicycle!

❓What were the first four-legged animals like?

Backboned land animals, such as Ichthyostega, evolved about 370 million years ago, from fish whose fins had become legs. They could crawl on to land, and they could breathe underwater, too.

Ichthyostega

Why did early land animals stay near water?

Ichthyostega and Acanthostega were ancestors of the amphibians, animals that lay their jelly-like eggs in water, and whose young live in water and have gills. As amphibians become adults, they lose their gills and develop lungs. They can live on land, but their skin and their eggs have to be kept damp, so they need to stay close to water.

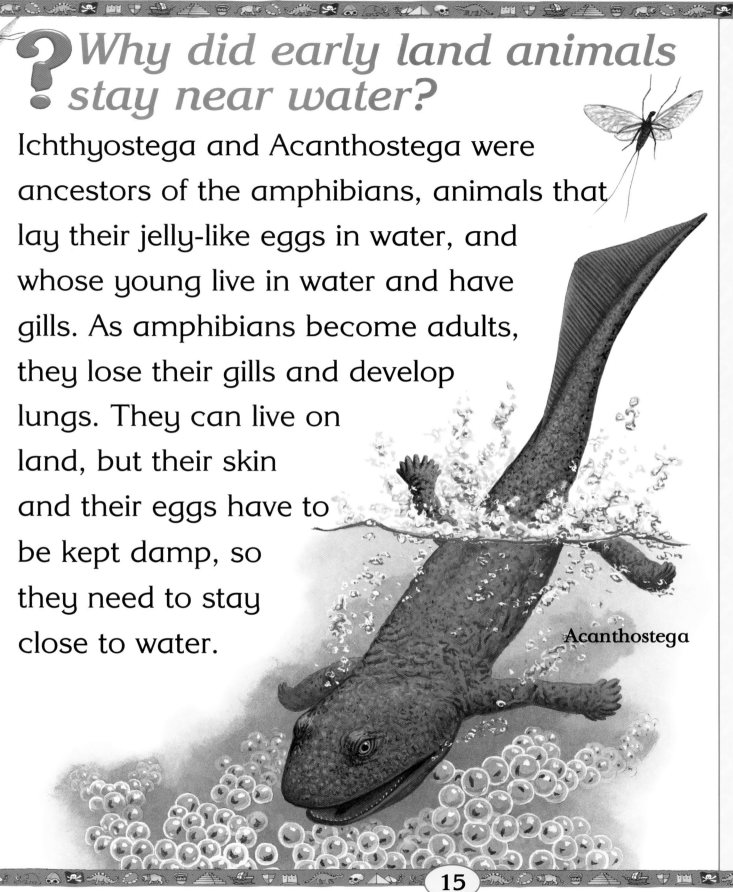

Acanthostega

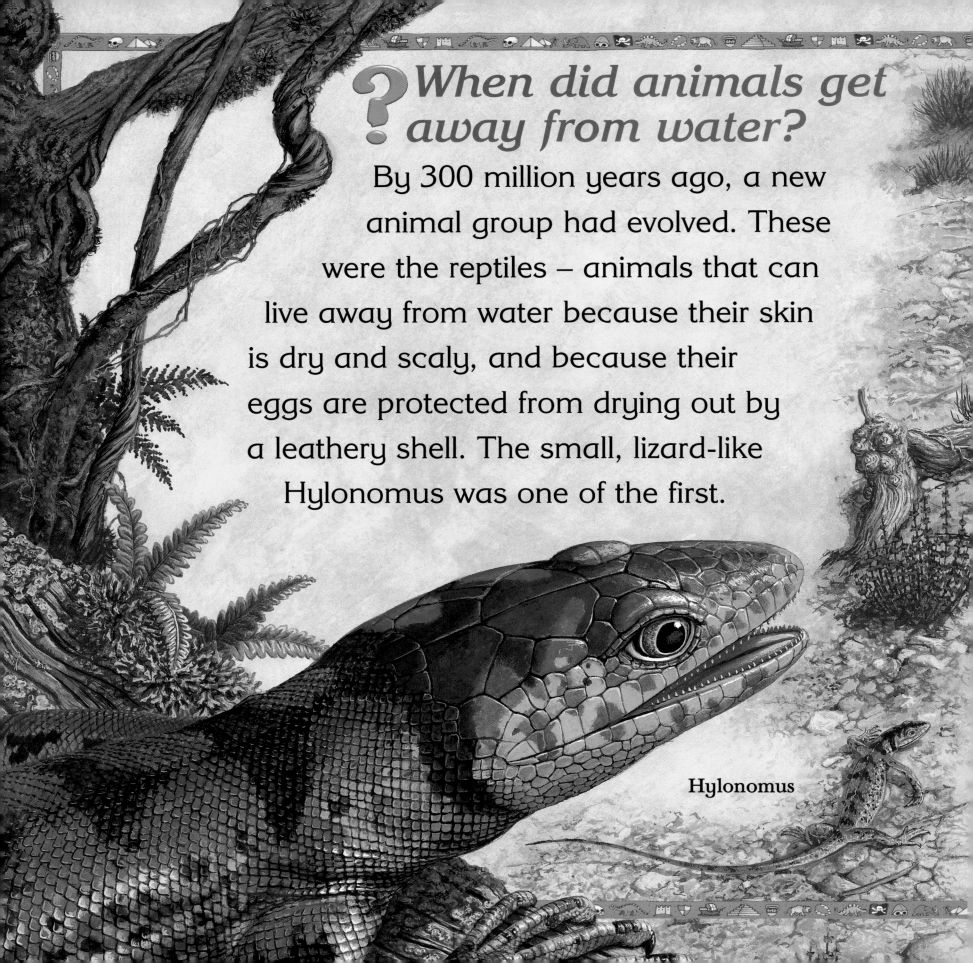

? When did animals get away from water?

By 300 million years ago, a new animal group had evolved. These were the reptiles – animals that can live away from water because their skin is dry and scaly, and because their eggs are protected from drying out by a leathery shell. The small, lizard-like Hylonomus was one of the first.

Hylonomus

Dimetrodon

❓ *What were the sailbacks?*

The sailbacks were reptiles and, like other reptiles, they were cold-blooded, with bodies that rely on the Sun's heat to warm them. Scientists think the sail-like fins on their backs worked rather like solar panels, soaking up heat. At 3 m from head to tail tip, Dimetrodon was as long as a car.

? Where did dinosaurs come from?

Dinosaurs evolved from a group called the ruling reptiles, which appeared about 250 million years ago – about 20 million years before the first dinosaurs.

Stagonolepis

? Where did crocodiles come from?

There's a good reason why today's crocodiles look a lot like early ruling reptiles – they also evolved from them. Scientists think one of the earliest, Deinosuchus, grew to a massive 15 m – three times as long as today's biggest crocodiles.

Deinosuchus

Chasmatosaurus

Lagosuchus

❓ *What was special about ruling reptiles?*

Early ones like Chasmatosaurus walked on all fours, but over time some ruling reptiles raised themselves up and began to walk on their back legs. The next stage after speedy, two-legged ruling reptiles like Lagosuchus was the dinosaur!

Who ruled the skies in dinosaur times?

Anurognathus

At about the same time as the first dinosaurs appeared, some reptiles evolved wings. These flying reptiles are called pterosaurs, and their wings were flaps of skin.

Pterodaustro

Dsungaripterus

What did pterosaurs eat?

Some pterosaurs snapped up insects, while others dived down to the sea to scoop up fish. Pterodaustro probably sieved tiny sea creatures through the bristly teeth in its lower jaw, much as flamingoes do today. Dsungaripterus may have used the tip of its curved beak to prize shellfish off rocks.

Quetzalcoatlus

? *Which pterosaur was as big as a hang-glider?*

The biggest pterosaur of all was Quetzalcoatlus. Scientists think its outspread wings measured a whopping 12 m – that gave it the biggest wings the world has ever known!

Pterodactylus

TRUE OR FALSE?

Pterosaurs had feathers.

FALSE. Most had furry bodies and leathery wings, as bats do today.

Some reptiles can fly today.

TRUE. There's a lizard that can glide on wing-like flaps of skin. There were lizard-like gliding reptiles in prehistoric times, too.

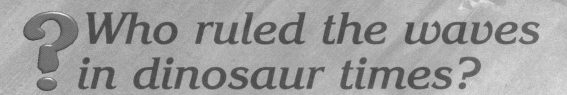

Who ruled the waves in dinosaur times?

While some reptiles took to the air, others went back to the oceans. By dinosaur times, three of the main groups were sea turtles, ichthyosaurs and the long-necked plesiosaurs.

Archelon

Which turtle was bigger than a rowing boat?

Archelon was more than 3.5 m long. Scientists think it ate jellyfish – it must have eaten truck-loads before it was full!

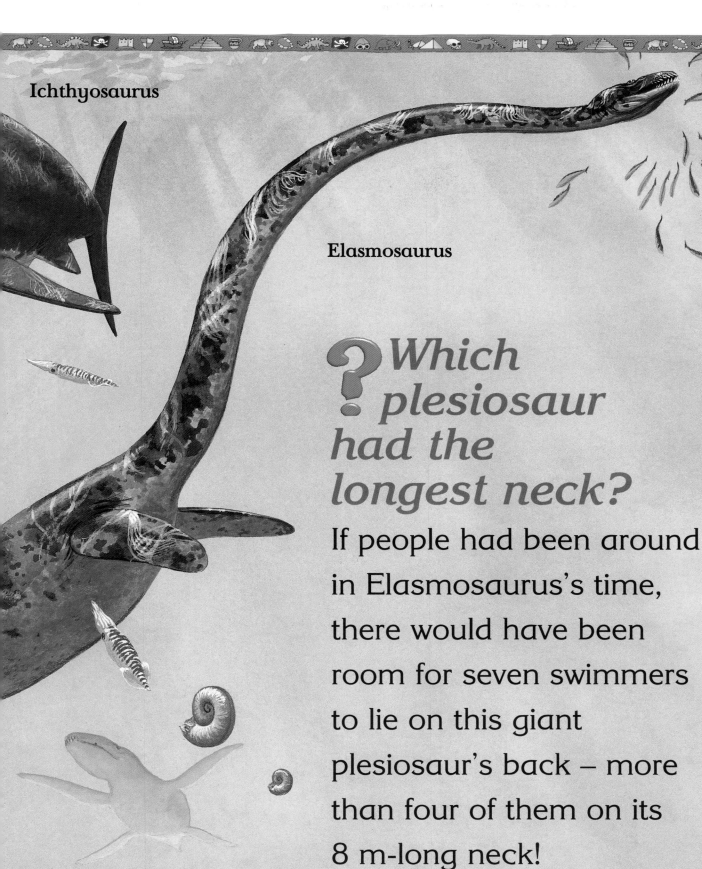

Ichthyosaurus

Elasmosaurus

? Which plesiosaur had the longest neck?

If people had been around in Elasmosaurus's time, there would have been room for seven swimmers to lie on this giant plesiosaur's back – more than four of them on its 8 m-long neck!

TRUE OR FALSE?

Plesiosaurs died out at the same time as the dinosaurs.

TRUE. The big sea reptiles died out 65 million years ago, as did the pterosaurs.

Plesiosaurs breathed underwater.

FALSE. The sea reptiles had to surface to breathe air, just as dolphins and whales do today.

❓ *What came after the dinosaurs?*

After the dinosaurs died out 65 million years ago, another group of animals, the mammals, began to take over. One of the special things about this group is that mammals feed their young on mother's milk. No other animals do this. Mammals evolved from reptiles, and they appeared about 220 million years ago. One of the earliest, Megazostrodon, was a little bigger than a mouse.

Zalambdalestes

Megazostrodon

Ptilodus

?Did early mammals lay eggs?

Although their young sucked milk, the first mammal mothers laid eggs. Over time, new kinds of mammal began to give birth to live young, just as most mammals do today. Egg-laying mammals are still around, though – Australia's duck-billed platypus is the most famous.

? Which were the first flying mammals?

Bats are still the only mammals that can flap their wings to fly. Unlike modern bats, though, the earliest-known bat had a long tail. It is called Icaronycteris, and it appeared about 54 million years ago.

Icaronycteris

Dinornis

? Which was the tallest bird?

At 3.5 m high, and a lot larger than a modern-day camel, Dinornis was the tallest bird that has ever lived. It belonged to a group of flightless New Zealand birds called moas, which died out about 200 years ago.

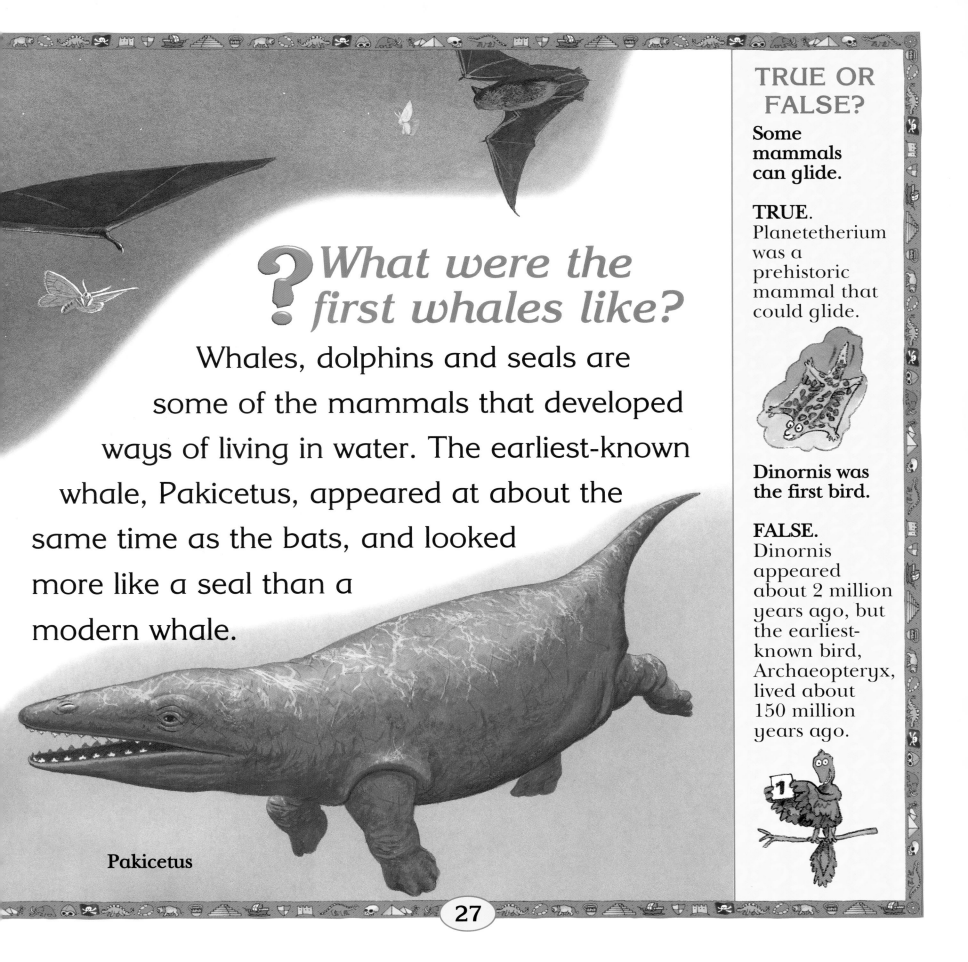

? *What were the first whales like?*

Whales, dolphins and seals are some of the mammals that developed ways of living in water. The earliest-known whale, Pakicetus, appeared at about the same time as the bats, and looked more like a seal than a modern whale.

Pakicetus

What were sabre-toothed cats like?

Their two huge fangs made sabre-tooths like Smilodon some of the fiercest cats that have ever lived. They could open their mouths really wide so they could stab their teeth into victims.

Smilodon

Which animals attacked sabre-tooths?

Packs of early wolves, called dire wolves, were brave enough to take on sabre-tooths. Scientists have found fossils of their bones covered in each other's teeth marks. Dire wolves and sabre-tooths lived about 25,000 years ago.

Dire wolves

? How big were the first bears?

Agriotherium lived about 5 million years ago. At 2 m long, it was about the same size as a modern grizzly bear.

Agriotherium

TRUE OR FALSE?

Dogs appeared 40 million years ago.

TRUE. But the earliest ones like Phlaocyon looked more like raccoons than the dogs you see today.

WOOF

Cats appeared 40 million years ago.

FALSE. They first appeared on Earth about 35 million years ago.

? Which was the biggest-ever land mammal?

Indricotherium

Indricotherium was as heavy as four elephants and 1.5 times the height of a modern giraffe. Although it looked like a cross between them, it was an early kind of rhinoceros.

? Which was the ugliest mammal?

Lots of prehistoric animals looked very strange in comparison to modern animals. With its lumpy, bumpy head, one of the weirdest-looking was Eobasileus.

Eobasileus

? *Which deer had branch-sized antlers?*

Megaloceros's antlers were massive – at 3.7 m across, they were wider than its body was long.

Megaloceros

Diatryma

❓ *When were horses the size of foxes?*

The earliest-known horse, Hyracotherium, had toes instead of hooves, and was only about 20 cm high. It evolved about 50 million years ago, and lived in forests, where its size helped it to hide from meat-eaters. Equus, the kind of horse we know today, didn't appear until about 5 million years ago.

Hyracotherium

When were elephants the size of pigs?

When the first elephants appeared about 40 million years ago, they were tiny. Moeritherium, for example, was only about 60 cm high. All sorts of strange-looking kinds evolved before the ancestors of modern elephants appeared about 5 million years ago.

Moeritherium

Deinotherium

Platybelodon

Anancus

?Why were mammoths woolly?

A mammoth's thick woolly fur was like a jumper, helping it to keep warm. Mammoths needed this extra layer because they lived during the Ice Ages – times when Earth's weather was so freezing cold that snow and ice spread down from the North Pole over Europe and North America.

Woolly mammoths

❓ *Why did mammoths die out?*

The last Ice Age began to end when the weather became warmer again about 12,000 years ago. Lots of animals died out at this time, including woolly mammoths and woolly rhinoceroses. Scientists think this happened partly because these animals couldn't cope with the warmer weather, but also because they were hunted by a new kind of mammal – human beings!

Woolly rhinoceros

Snow hare

TRUE OR FALSE?

Scientists have found frozen mammoths.

TRUE. In 1977, they even found a baby mammoth's body in the frozen ground of Siberia. It died 40,000 years ago.

All mammoths were big.

FALSE. Mini-mammoths lived on an island in the Arctic Ocean. They died out about 6,000 years ago.

Which dinosaur was a bighead?

and other questions about dinosaurs

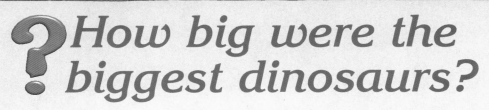

? *How big were the biggest dinosaurs?*

Long-necked dinosaurs, such as Brachiosaurus, were massive. Measuring more than 22 m from head to tail, and weighing well over 30 tonnes, this dinosaur was about as long as a tennis court and heavier than five elephants. It was tall enough to peer over the top of a four-storey house!

Brachiosaurus

? How small were the smallest dinosaurs?

Some dinosaurs were tiny. At about 1 m long, for example, Compsognathus wasn't much larger than a turkey!

Compsognathus

TRUE OR FALSE?

Brachiosaurus was the biggest dinosaur of all.

FALSE. Other long-necked dinosaurs were even larger – Argentinosaurus may have been twice as big.

Dinosaurs were the biggest animals ever.

FALSE. The blue whale is the biggest animal ever, at 130 tonnes.

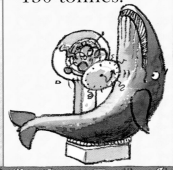

? How many kinds of dinosaur were there?

Dinosaurs were around for millions of years, and all sorts of different kinds developed. Scientists have now named about 800 dinosaurs, but there may have been twice as many kinds altogether.

When did dinosaurs live?

The very first kinds of dinosaur appeared on Earth about 225 million years ago. One of the earliest was Herrerasaurus, a meat-eater that lived in the area we now call Argentina.

What sort of animal were they?

Dinosaurs were reptiles, but they were a bit different from other reptiles such as lizards, crocodiles and tortoises. Dinosaurs held their legs straight under their bodies – unlike other reptiles, whose legs sprawl out to the side.

TRUE OR FALSE?

Dinosaurs could fly.

FALSE. They were land animals. Other creatures ruled the air and the seas.

Dinosaur babies hatched from eggs.

TRUE. Like other reptiles, dinosaurs laid eggs.

? How do we know about dinosaurs?

No one knows exactly what dinosaurs were like because, about 65 million years ago, they all suddenly died out. Scientists work like detectives to piece bits of information together, and their main clues are fossils – the stony remains of living things that died a very long time ago.

? How were fossils made?

Sometimes a dead animal would sink to the bottom of a river, lake or sea, where it was covered by sand or mud. Over millions of years, the sand and mud became rock, and the animal's bones turned into fossils.

What kind of dinosaur fossils do scientists find?

The most common dinosaur fossils formed from hard body parts such as bones and teeth. Sometimes, though, scientists find fossils of dinosaur eggs or droppings, or rocks that show the pattern of their skin or footprints.

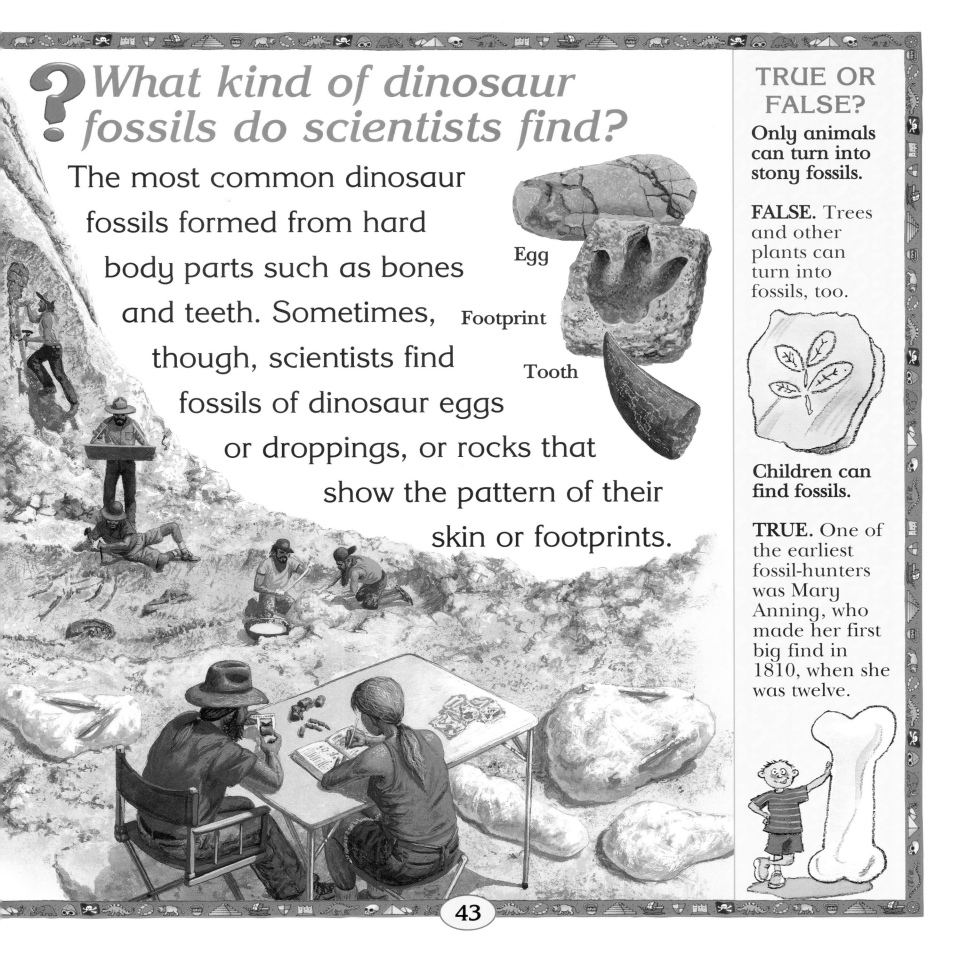

Egg

Footprint

Tooth

TRUE OR FALSE?

Only animals can turn into stony fossils.

FALSE. Trees and other plants can turn into fossils, too.

Children can find fossils.

TRUE. One of the earliest fossil-hunters was Mary Anning, who made her first big find in 1810, when she was twelve.

What did dinosaurs eat?

Most dinosaurs ate plants. There were lots of fierce and hungry meat-eaters, though, and they ate anything they could catch, including other dinosaurs!

Pine-trees

Ginkgo

Magnolia

Why do scientists love dinosaur droppings?

It's lucky that fossils don't smell, because scientists study fossilised dinosaur droppings to find out about the kind of things dinosaurs liked to eat.

Did dinosaurs eat grass?

Cycad

No, not even plant-eating dinosaurs ate grass, because these plants didn't appear until long after the dinosaurs died out. Plant-eating dinosaurs mainly ate ferns and early kinds of tree, such as the palm-like cycad, and pine trees.

Dinosaurs ate flowers.

TRUE. Flowers first appeared about 135 million years ago, so the later dinosaurs may have liked eating them.

Some dinosaurs were cannibals.

TRUE. Scientists have discovered a fossilised Coelophysis that had eaten its own babies.

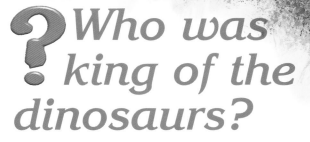 *Who was king of the dinosaurs?*

Rex means 'king', and Tyrannosaurus means 'tyrant lizard' (a tyrant is a cruel, powerful ruler). Scientists named Tyrannosaurus rex because they thought it was big and mean enough to rule over all other animals, killing and eating anything it fancied. At about 12 m, it was bus-sized, with a huge head and a mouth big enough to gulp you down whole.

Tyrannosaurus rex

What colour was Tyrannosaurus?

No one has found a fossil that shows what colour any of the dinosaurs were. Scientists think that some were brightly coloured, while others were patterned to match their surroundings – just as many animals are today.

Giganotosaurus

Who was the giant dinosaur?

Giganotosaurus means 'giant southern lizard', and scientists think that this meat-eater was even bigger than Tyrannosaurus!

? *Which dinosaur went fishing?*

At about 10.5 m long, Baryonyx was a big dinosaur with crocodile-like jaws. Scientists think it ate fish, snapping them up in its mouth or hooking them up out of the water with its thumb claws, just as grizzly bears do today.

Baryonyx

Suchomimus

Which dinosaur had a sail on its back?

No one is certain what the sail-like structure on Spinosaurus's back was for. It may have been used like a flag to signal to other dinosaurs, or it may have worked a bit like a solar panel to help Spinosaurus heat up or cool down.

Spinosaurus

Who was the biggest fish-eater?

Suchomimus was at least a metre longer than its cousin Baryonyx, and probably grew to as long as the 12-m Tyrannosaurus.

? Which dinosaur had a long big toenail?

Velociraptor was one of the scariest dinosaurs in the 1993 movie Jurassic Park. This dinosaur didn't just have sharp teeth and vicious clawed hands. Even more frightening was the huge curved claw on each foot – when Velociraptor attacked, it could swing these claws forwards, to slash at its prey.

Velociraptors

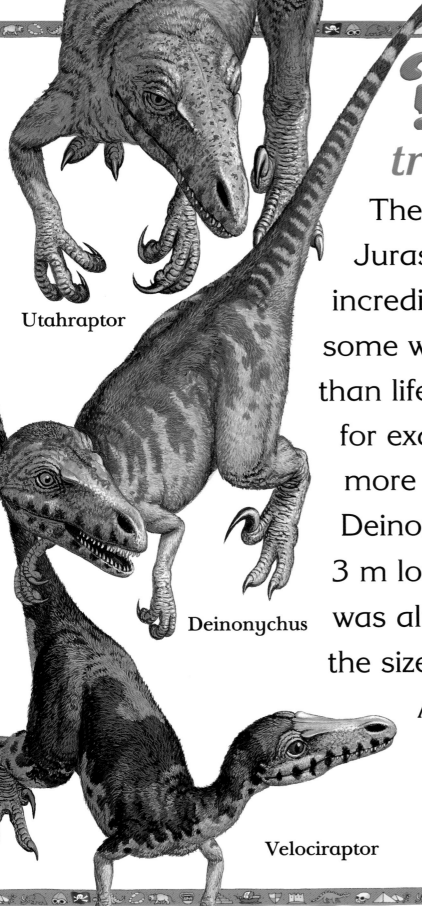

Utahraptor

Deinonychus

Velociraptor

？*Are model dinosaurs true to life?*

The model dinosaurs in Jurassic Park were incredibly realistic, but some were a little larger than life. The Velociraptors, for example, looked more like their cousin, Deinonychus. At about 3 m long, this dinosaur was almost twice the size of Velociraptor. And another cousin, Utahraptor, was twice as big as Deinonychus!

Diplodocus

?Which dinosaurs cracked a whip?

The huge plant-eating dinosaurs didn't just have long necks – some of them also had incredibly long tails. Apatosaurus, Barosaurus and Diplodocus may have flicked their extra-long tails like a whip, making an incredibly loud noise to scare away their enemies.

Allosaurus

Why did the long-necked dinosaurs eat stones?

The long-necked dinosaurs couldn't chew their tough plant food. To get at the goodness, they swallowed stones which rubbed together in their tummies to mash the plants into a mush.

Brain

Stomach

Were long-necked dinosaurs brainy?

The long-necked dinosaurs had tiny brains in comparison to their huge bodies. Because of this, scientists think they were among the least intelligent of the dinosaurs.

TRUE OR FALSE?

Long-necked dinosaurs were very greedy.

TRUE. They were so big that to stay alive, they had to spend nearly all their time eating.

Tyrannosaurus rex was the brainiest dinosaur.

FALSE. It was brainier than long-necked dinosaurs, but not as smart as a Velociraptor.

Which dinosaurs had duckbills?

Parasaurolophus, Corythosaurus and Lambeosaurus belonged to a group of plant-eating dinosaurs called duckbills – named because their mouths ended in a toothless beak, or bill. When predators threatened them, they could run away on two legs, and may have rushed into the water to escape.

Parasaurolophus

Saurolophus

Tsintaosaurus

Corythosaurus

? Who liked to blow his own trumpet?

Parasaurolophus had a weird, hollow crest bone, which it may have blown through like a trumpet. Scientists made a model of the bone, and found it produced a low booming sound.

Air space

Lambeosaurus

? Who was the helmet lizard?

Corythosaurus means 'helmet lizard', even though this dinosaur's crest looked more like a dinner plate than a helmet! Scientists think the duckbilled dinosaurs used their crests to show off when trying to attract a mate.

? Were dinosaurs good parents?

Maiasaura means 'good mother lizard', and scientists named this dinosaur because they found it beside a nest full of its babies. Other kinds of dinosaur may have also stayed with their young, feeding and protecting them.

Maiasaura

? Which dinosaur laid the biggest egg?

Some of the biggest eggs found so far belonged to a long-necked dinosaur called Hypselosaurus. They were about 30 cm long – roughly the same size as a rugby ball.

Oviraptor

Dinosaur eggs were first found in the 1800s.

FALSE. The first eggs were found in the 1920s. They belonged to a Protoceratops.

Dinosaurs used to nest in trees.

FALSE. They made their nests on the ground. Some nests were holes, others were built up into mounds.

? Which of the dinosaurs was an egg robber?

Oviraptor means 'egg robber', and this dinosaur also got its name because it was discovered near a nest. Scientists used to think it was about to steal the eggs when it died. Later they found a fossilised Oviraptor that had died protecting its own nest, proving it was a good parent, after all.

Why did Triceratops have horns?

Triceratops was like a giant rhinoceros – as heavy as an elephant and as long as a truck. Even though it looked so fierce, Triceratops was a plant-eater and probably used its horns to scare off meat-eating enemies, such as Tyrannosaurus rex and Velociraptor.

Triceratops

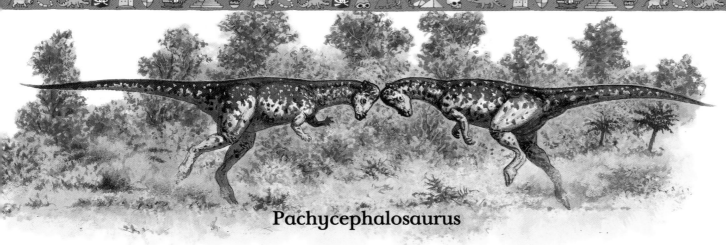

Pachycephalosaurus

 Who were headbangers?

Pachycephalosaurus's skull was so thick and tough that scientists think it worked like a crash helmet, and that these dinosaurs fought each other by headbanging.

Pentaceratops

Which dinosaur was a bighead?

Triceratops's head was about 2 m long, but its cousin Pentaceratops's was bigger. At over 3 m, even a car could have parked on it!

Triceratops could sharpen its own teeth.

TRUE. When it chewed, its teeth ground together and got sharper.

Dinosaurs only lived in small groups.

FALSE. Some, including Triceratops, lived in large herds made up of dozens of dinosaurs.

? Why were some dinosaurs built like tanks?

Hylaeosaurus

Some plant-eating dinosaurs, such as Sauropelta, were big bruisers with extra-tough skin covered in bony spikes and bumps. All this armour-plating helped protect them against meat-eaters.

Polacanthus

Sauropelta

Which dinosaur spiked its enemies?

Stegosaurus's tail had vicious spikes at its tip, which were just as dangerous as Triceratops's horns.

Stegosaurus

Which dinosaur packed a mean punch?

When Euoplocephalus swung its tail, the bumps on its tip worked like a club for bashing its enemies about. Ouch!

? How fast could dinosaurs run?

Scientists think that dinosaurs such as Gallimimus and Struthiomimus were the speediest, and that they could run as fast as ostriches. Ostriches can't fly, but they are the largest birds alive today – with their long, strong legs they can belt across the ground at speeds of up to 65 kph.

Struthiomimus

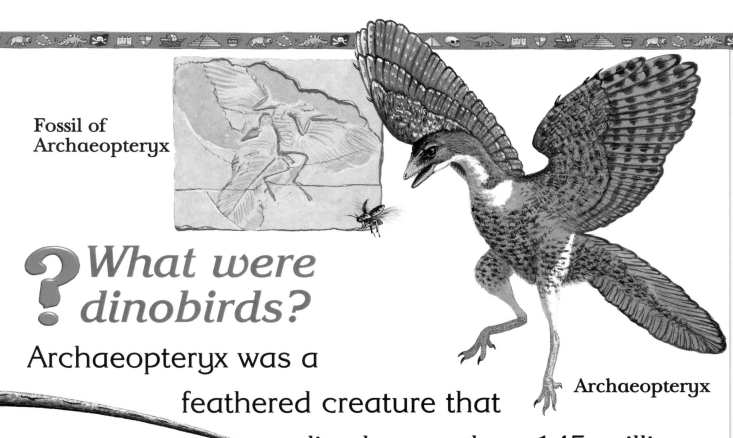

Fossil of Archaeopteryx

Archaeopteryx

?What were dinobirds?

Archaeopteryx was a feathered creature that lived more than 145 million years ago. Many scientists now think that birds are descended from dinosaurs, and that Archaeopteryx was a cross between a bird and a dinosaur – a dinobird!

What happened to the dinosaurs?

Many scientists think that 65 million years ago, a gigantic chunk of space rock smashed into the Earth. The force of the hit was like an explosion. It threw up huge clouds of dust which blocked out the Sun and plunged the Earth into freezing darkness. Without sunlight, plants couldn't grow, so first the plant-eating dinosaurs died of cold and hunger, then the meat-eaters starved.

?Are any dinosaurs alive today?

No dinosaurs survived the disaster, but some birds did. So if scientists are right, and birds are descended from dinosaurs, then their relatives are still alive and hopping today!

Robin

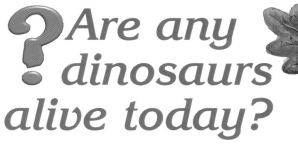

Who were the first people?

and other questions about early people

? Who were the first people?

The scientific name for people like you and me is Homo sapiens, and our ancestors, the first modern humans, appeared about 180,000 years ago. Experts believe that, like all creatures, we evolved very, very slowly, over millions of years, from earlier kinds of animal.

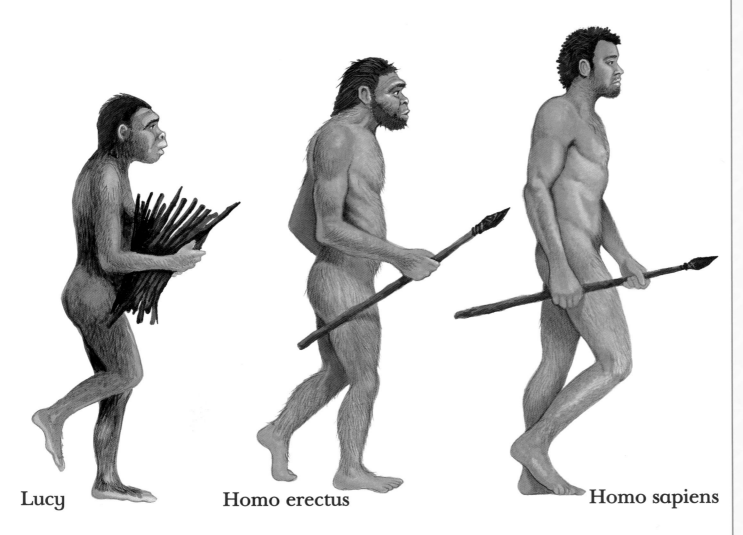

Lucy Homo erectus Homo sapiens

❓ *Who was Lucy?*

The earliest human-like creatures were the Australopithecines, who were evolving as long as 4.5 million years ago. Lucy is the nickname given to a fossilised Australopithecine skeleton found in 1974.

What was the Stone Age?

Well over 2.5 million years ago, some bright spark picked up a rock and made a stone tool from it. When experts talk about the Stone Age, they mean the long period of time from making the first stone tools to about 5,000 years ago, when bronze tools were first made.

What were early tools used for?

Homo erectus people chipped stones into sharp hand-axes, which they mainly used for skinning animals and cutting up the meat.

When were weapons invented?

The earliest weapons were pointed wooden sticks used as hunting spears. It's likely that Homo erectus people were the first to make them, more than 400,000 years ago.

? Why were Stone Age people great travellers?

Although the first human-like creatures lived in eastern and southern Africa, by about 1.8 million years ago, Homo erectus people were exploring other lands. It wasn't long before some of them reached southeastern Asia. By 700,000 years ago, others were living in Europe.

Homo erectus people

? Who were the first Americans?

Some of our modern human ancestors were living in North America by 15,000 years ago. They were able to walk there from northern Asia because it was once joined to North America by dry land called Beringia.

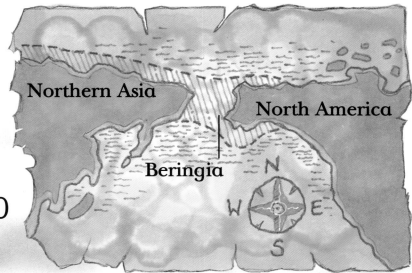

Northern Asia

North America

Beringia

N W E S

? Which bright sparks lit the first fires?

Experts think that Homo erectus people were the first to toast their toes around a camp fire, perhaps as long as 1.6 million years ago.

? Why was fire useful?

The weather got colder once Homo erectus headed out of sunny Africa, so fire must have been one way of keeping warm. Stone Age people also cooked over fires and hardened their wooden spear-tips in the flames.

How did Stone Age people light fires?

The first fire-makers probably took flames from bush fires started by a flash of lightning. Later on, people sparked off their own fires by rubbing dry sticks together or bashing two stones against each other.

Homo erectus family

Neanderthals

❓ Who were the Neanderthals?

The Neanderthals were a kind of early human who evolved several thousand years before our modern human ancestors appeared.

Neanderthal man

❓ Were Neanderthal people stupid?

Experts once thought so, but they've changed their minds. The Neanderthals looked different from our ancestors – they were sturdier, with differently shaped heads – but they seem to have been just as skilful.

Neanderthals hunting
woolly mammoths

? *How did Neanderthals hunt with fire?*

Some Neanderthals lived through

the Ice Ages – long periods of freezing

weather when much of Europe and North

America was covered in snow and ice.

Mammoths were huge, so the Neanderthals had

to invent clever ways of killing them, like using

burning branches to chase them over cliffs.

TRUE OR FALSE?

There are Neanderthals around today.

FALSE. No one knows why, but they died out about 30,000 years ago.

Neanderthals lived in North America.

FALSE. They died out before the first people travelled there.

What other animals did people hunt?

Stone Age hunters went after anything they could catch – from mammoths and rhinoceroses, to herds of reindeer and bison. People who lived by the sea caught seals and fish, while the first Australians hunted giant kangaroos.

Reindeer

Wolf

Bison

Bear

❓How did people cook?

Some time after they learned to use fire, Stone Age people invented spits for cooking roast dinners. Early spits were probably made by pushing a sharp stick through a piece of meat, then balancing the stick on forked twigs.

❓Did they have cooking pots?

Most Stone Age people didn't. Clay pots weren't made until about 11,000 years ago.

? Did Stone Age people live in caves?

They did if they were near mountains or cliffs and could find a big enough cave. Stone Age people lived in bands made up of several families, and a small band might have 25 members.

Why did mammoths come in handy?

The people who didn't live near mountains or cliffs built their own shelters. Some were dome-shaped huts made from mammoth bones and tusks.

Mammoth hut

Did Stone Age people build villages?

Not until about 10,000 years ago. Before then, people spent much of their time on the move, looking for food. These kind of travellers are called hunter-gatherers, because they lived by hunting animals and gathering plants to eat.

Cave painting

?Who were the first artists?

Some time around 30,000 years ago, our modern human ancestors began to carve and paint pictures into cave walls and roofs. Most pictures were of the animals they hunted – everything from a charging bison, to a herd of leaping deer.

❓ *What paints did they use?*

Cave artists used kinds of earth called ochre for yellow, red and brown. Clay or chalky stones gave them white, while burnt twigs gave them charcoal for black. They dabbed the paint on with their fingers, or made brushes by fixing pads of animal fur to sticks. Sometimes they spray-painted by blowing paint through a hollow bone.

❓ *Who were the first musicians?*

No one knows when music began, but the world's oldest musical instrument is a whistle carved from an animal bone more than 60,000 years ago!

Stone Age musician

?Were Stone Age people religious?

In Stone Age times, anything mysterious or powerful must have seemed like a god or goddess – from the Sun, Moon and stars, to fire, wind, water and animals.

?Did they have priests?

We don't know for sure, but some sculptures and cave paintings show mysterious beings that are part-human, part-animal. These may have been early priests who dressed as animals for special ceremonies.

Religious ceremony

Stone Age skull

Medical instruments

? Did they have doctors?

Not like the doctors of today, but they did try their hand at operations. People have found 8,000-year-old skulls with holes – Stone Age doctors probably thought illnesses were caused by evil spirits, and cut the neat little holes to let them escape.

Stone Age people probably believed there was a heaven.

TRUE. Late Stone Age people buried their dead with all sorts of things that would be useful in an afterlife.

They took pills when they were sick.

FALSE. But they probably knew how to use plants to cure things like upset tummies.

?How do we know what clothes were like?

We think the first clothes were made from animal skins because we've found tools for cleaning the skins, and we know that looms for weaving cloth weren't invented until about 7,000 years ago.

Making clothes

We haven't found any early clothes, though, because unlike bones or stone tools, leather rots away quickly. Some of the earliest clothing finds came from the graves of people buried in Russia about 25,000 years ago.

Who was the Iceman?

In 1991, a mummified body complete with clothes, weapons and even a backpack was discovered frozen into the ice of the Alps mountains. The mummy was nicknamed the Iceman, and it's one of the oldest ever found. When he died about 5,300 years ago, the Iceman was wearing a leather tunic and shoes, a furry hat and a woven grass cape.

The Iceman

? Did people wear jewellery?

People were wearing beautiful jewellery by the time the first cave art was created. Polished stones, shells, ivory and animal teeth were all made into bracelets, necklaces and headbands.

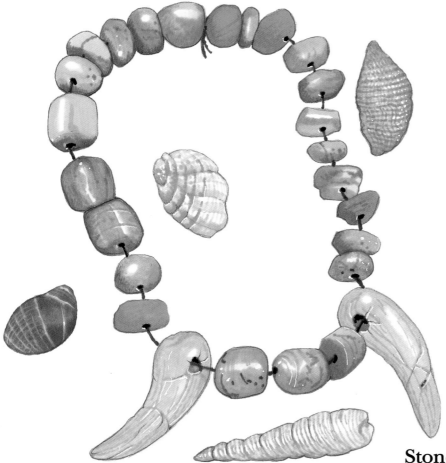

Stone Age necklace

? Did they carry lucky charms?

We've also found beautiful small carvings of animals, which people probably carried about with them as lucky charms.

Carved animals may have been toys or charms.

Did they cut their hair?

They probably did, but not with scissors – they weren't invented until long after the Stone Age was over. A 25,000-year-old ivory carving shows a beautiful woman who looks as though her hair was cut into a fringe.

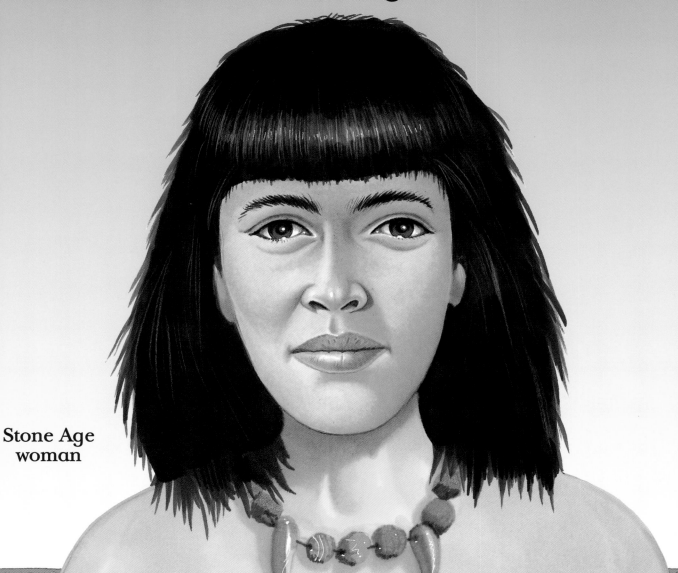

Stone Age woman

Who were the first farmers?

In the Middle East by 10,000 years ago, people were settling down. Instead of moving about as hunter-gatherers, they saved wild seeds so they could grow their own crops, and built villages where they could live all the time. Later on, they started to keep animals. Farming had begun.

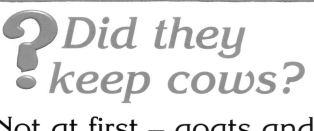 Did they keep cows?

Not at first – goats and sheep were the first animals to be farmed. Pigs and cows were tamed and farmed a while later.

Did they have pets?

Dogs have long been people's best friends. Their ancestors were wild wolves, which people began taming to help them hunt a few hundred years before villages were built.

Tamed wolves helped hunters.

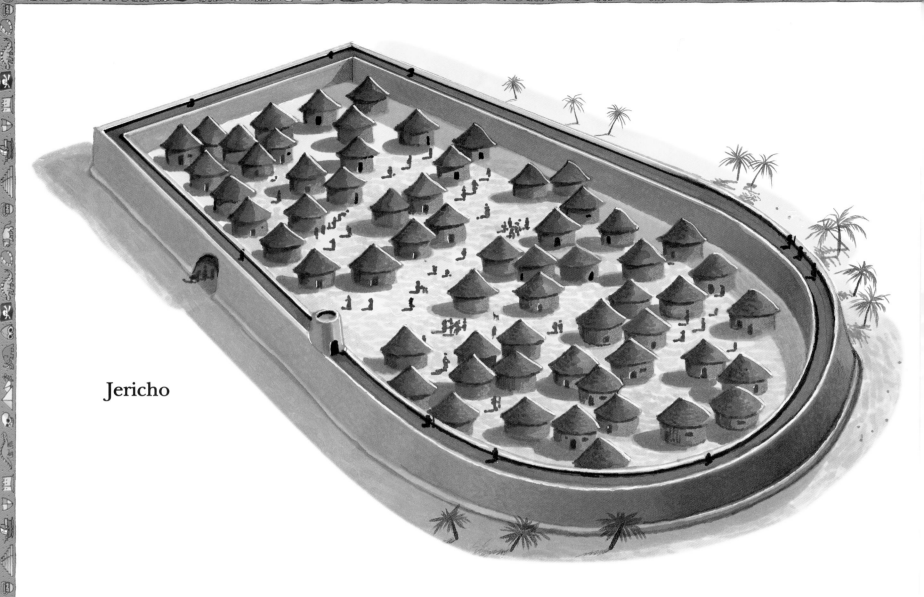

Jericho

❓ *When were the first towns built?*

In some places, farmers were so successful that their villages grew into towns. The earliest we know about is Jericho in the Middle East. By about 9,000 years ago, it was surrounded by high stone walls and a deep ditch.

❓ *How big were they?*

Jericho was home to at least 2,000 people, but around three times as many were living in Çatalhöyük in Turkey by 7,000 years ago. Unlike Jericho, with its bee-hive houses, Çatalhöyük was a warren of mud-brick boxes, with doors on the roof tops.

Çatalhöyük

When were the first cities built?

The first cities had grown up by 5,000 years ago, at the very end of the Stone Age. They were built by the people of Sumer, a land in the Middle East, and they were huge, with homes for tens of thousands of citizens.

What were they like?

At the heart of Sumerian cities like Ur were huge temples called ziggurats. All around were narrow winding streets packed with houses, shops and inns.

Ziggurat

? *What was special about the Sumerians?*

The Sumerians were great inventors, and their most useful brainwave was coming up with the first proper writing. It's hard piecing together how Stone Age people lived because there were no written records. But from Sumerian times on, we start to get everything from histories to love poems and shopping lists.

Sumerian writing tablet

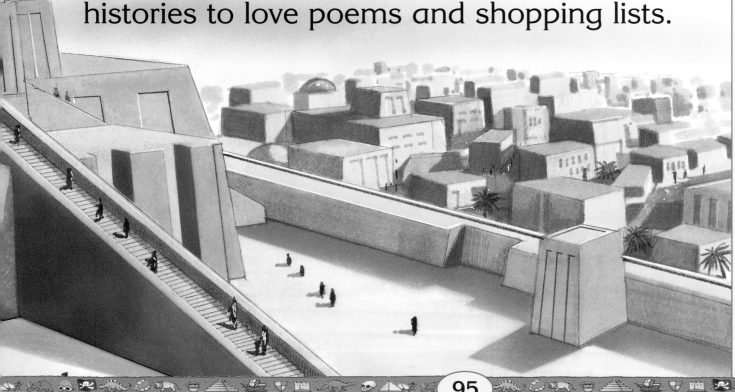

How were mummies made?

and other questions about early civilizations

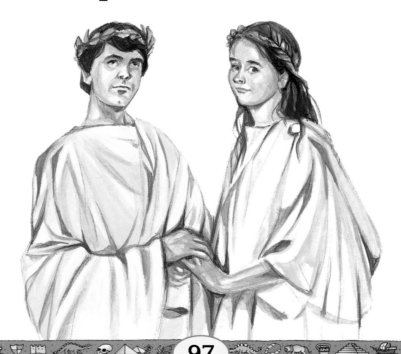

Who built the pyramids?

The pyramids were built by the Ancient Egyptians as magnificent tombs for their kings, the pharaohs, and other very important people. The biggest is the Great Pyramid at Giza. It was 146.5 m high when it was built – taller than the Statue of Liberty is today.

Why did pharaohs need pyramids?

No one is certain, but we do know that the Egyptians believed the dead travelled to another world, the Afterlife. The sloping sides of the pyramids may have been like lauch ramps, helping the pharaohs to shoot up to heaven.

Why were the Egyptians ancient?

We call them ancient because they lived so long ago – the Great Pyramid was finished in 2550 BC (before Christ was born – AD means after Christ's birth).

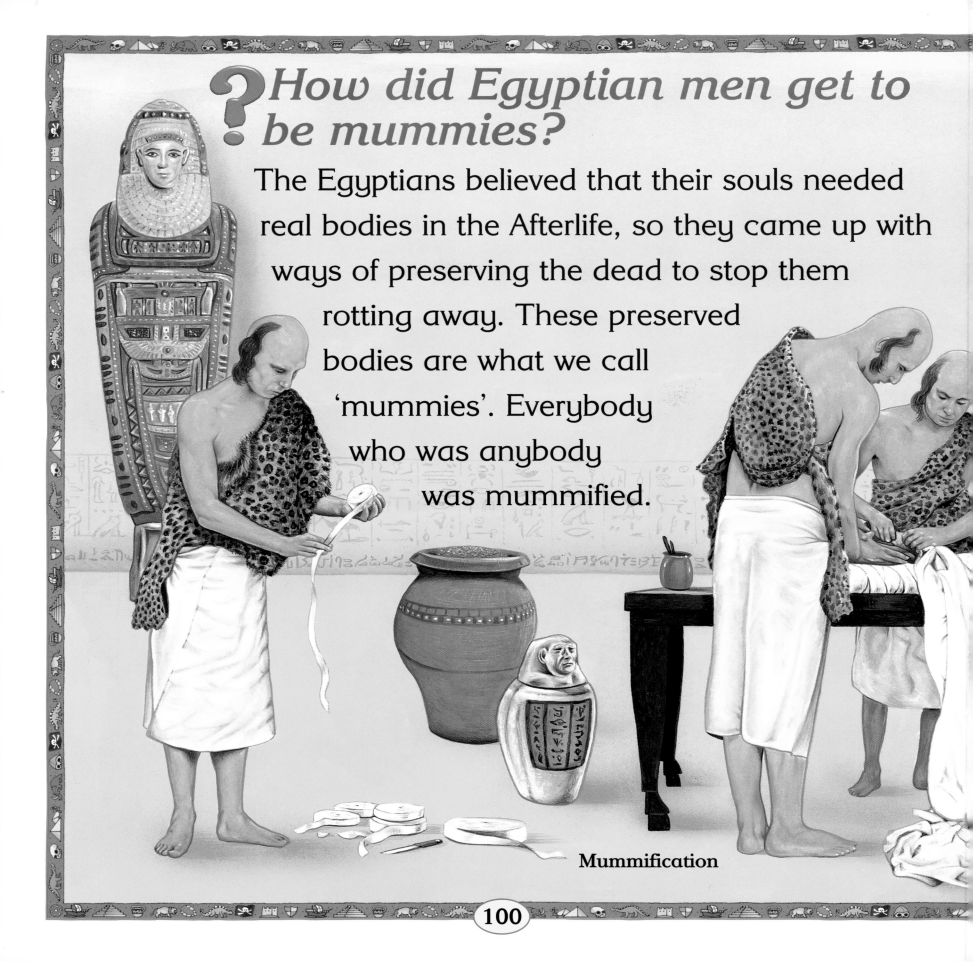

?How did Egyptian men get to be mummies?

The Egyptians believed that their souls needed real bodies in the Afterlife, so they came up with ways of preserving the dead to stop them rotting away. These preserved bodies are what we call 'mummies'. Everybody who was anybody was mummified.

Mummification

? *How were mummies made?*

The first stage in making a mummy was taking out the brain, lungs, heart, stomach, intestines and liver. Then the body was washed and left to dry out for 40 days in salty stuff called natron. Next up was a rub down in special oils. Finally, the body was carefully wrapped in linen bandages and put inside a nest of coffins.

❓ Who was Tutankhamun?

Tutankhamun was only 17 when he died, but he's become Egypt's best-known pharaoh. He isn't famous for what he did when he was alive, but for the glittering treasures that were buried with him – including a magnificent gold face mask and a solid gold coffin!

Tutankhamun's mask

Ancient Egyptian party

❓ Did Egyptians throw good parties?

Pharaohs and rich people threw amazing parties, where they feasted on beef and antelope meat, and drank fine wines. There was entertainment too, from musicians, singers, dancers acrobats and even magicians.

Gazelle hunt

❓ *Who hunted hippos?*

Rich Egyptian men did – they loved taking a boat out on the River Nile to hunt hippos and crocodiles. Another favourite sport was taking a racing chariot out into the desert to hunt lions, gazelles and ostriches.

❓ *What were Egyptian homes like?*

Egyptian house

Egypt is a hot country where it hardly ever rains, so houses didn't need pointed roofs for rain to run off. Bricks were made from river mud mixed with straw and reed. Ordinary people's homes were quite small and simple, but rich people's were big with lots of rooms and a garden.

Greek soldiers

Egyptian soldiers

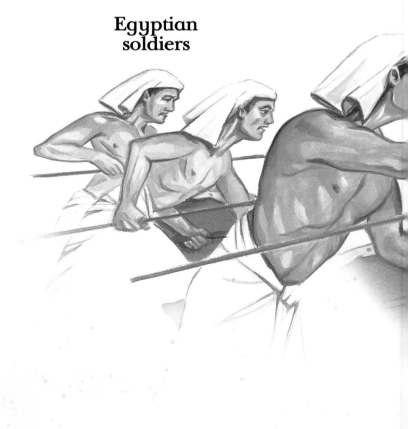

❓ *Did children go to school?*

Boys from rich families did and, like you, they had to learn to read and write. Egyptians wrote using picture symbols called hieroglyphs, and boys had to learn 700 of them off by heart.

Egyptian children

❓ *What happened to the Egyptians?*

Although the Ancient Egyptians were once the most powerful nation in the world, by about 1000 BC their days of greatness were over. In 332 BC, Egypt was conquered by the Ancient Greeks and made part of their empire.

Slaves had to water the Hanging Gardens of Babylon by hand, because they were created before hose pipes were invented!

The Colossus of Rhodes was a huge bronze statue of the Greek sun god Helios. It was about as high as today's Statue of Liberty in New York.

?What were the Seven Wonders?

The Seven Wonders were the top spots for tourists to visit in ancient times. They were built more than 2,200 years ago.

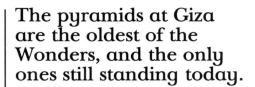

The pyramids at Giza are the oldest of the Wonders, and the only ones still standing today.

The gold and ivory Statue of Zeus at Olympia was over six times as high as a man.

The Lighthouse at Alexandria was more than 120 m high. The fire burning at its top could be seen by sailors far out at sea.

The Temple of Artemis at Ephesus was one of the largest temples of the ancient world.

After the pyramids, the huge Mausoleum at Halicarnassus was the most famous tomb of ancient times.

Most of the Wonders were designed by the Ancient Greeks.

TRUE. The Greeks made them all, except the Hanging Gardens and the pyramids.

The world's first zoo was in Alexandria.

TRUE. It had a leopard, a python, a giraffe and a polar bear.

? Who were the Ancient Greeks?

By 700 BC, the Greek world was made up of lots of separate city-states, each formed from a city and the surrounding farmland. The biggest and most powerful city-states were Athens and Sparta.

? Did the Greeks have armies?

They certainly did! The city-states were a quarrelsome lot and they often went to war. Only Sparta had a full-time army, though. The other city-states called freemen to arms when a war broke out.

Athenian soldiers

❓*Did they have kings?*

Most city-states were ruled by a king or a group of wealthy men at first. However, one of the Greeks' main claims to fame is the invention of people power. Democracy is a system of government in which people vote on how their country is run, and it was first put into practice in Athens in 508 BC.

Voting in Athens

Spartan soldiers

Athenian women helped to run cities.

FALSE. Only freemen over the age of 17 did – women and slaves weren't allowed to vote.

The biggest city-states all had navies.

TRUE. Greek warships had a vicious metal spike in front – the idea was to ram and sink enemy ships.

What did Greeks eat for breakfast?

Porridge was a favourite at breakfast time, made with barley instead of oats and livened up with figs. Lunch was usually bread and goat's cheese, while dinner might be a tasty pigeon or chicken, with fresh fruit for pudding.

Who were the toughest Greeks?

Spartan training camp

The Spartans were as tough as nails. Instead of going to ordinary school, boys were taken away from their mothers and sent to army training camps at just seven years old. To harden them up, they were kept cold and hungry and forced to go barefoot.

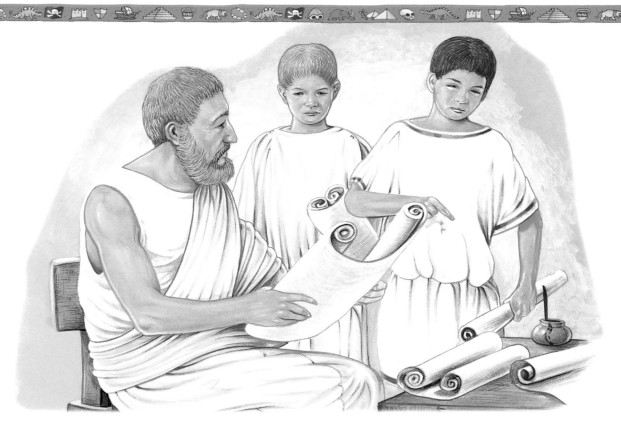

Greek babies had potties.

TRUE. But Greek potties were made of pottery, not plastic!

Spartan girls were softies.

FALSE. Girls learnt to run, jump and wrestle, to toughen them up for having babies later on.

❓*What did children learn at school?*

Only Greek boys went to school – girls stayed at home and learnt how to run a household. School subjects included reading, writing, maths, music, athletics and public speaking. Schooling began when boys were 6 or 7, and lasted until they were 18-20 years old.

❓ *When were the Olympics first held?*

The first Olympic Games were held in 776 BC, to honour Zeus, the chief of the Greek gods. They were held every four years, and thousands of athletes came from all over Greece to take part.

❓ *Were there swimming races?*

No, the Greek Olympic events were running, boxing, wrestling, javelin and discus throwing, the long jump, horse racing and chariot racing.

❓ *Did athletes win medals?*

No – winners were given small prizes at the Games, such as a crown of laurel leaves or a jar of olive oil. They were treated like superstars and showered with gifts and food when they got home, though.

Olympic champion

❓ Why did the Greeks laugh at frogs?

One of the smash hit theatre plays in Ancient Greek times was Frogs by the playwright Aristophanes. The Greeks were the first people to build theatres and put on plays. The theatres were open air, and the actors were all men, wearing masks painted to show which character they were playing.

Philosophers

Greek theatre

Why were the Greeks wise?

The Greeks were great thinkers, who developed the art of philosophy – thinking about big questions such as the meaning of life. The most important Greek philosophers were Socrates, Plato and Aristotle.

Why was Alexander great?

Alexander the Great was a brilliant Greek general, who won a huge empire in the early 300s BC. This was the peak of Greek power. In 146 BC, the Romans took over Greece and made it part of their own empire.

Alexander the Great

? When was Stonehenge built?

Local tribespeople began building the great stone circles of Stonehenge in southern England in about 2100 BC. The circles were built in stages, and took a lot of hard work and hundreds of years to finish – the biggest stones weigh as much as ten elephants! Experts think the tribes used Stonehenge for religious ceremonies, perhaps for worshipping the Sun and the Moon.

Stonehenge

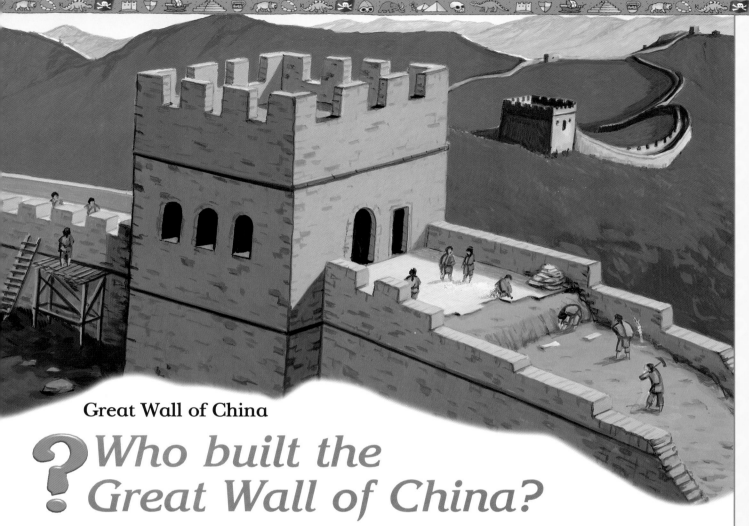

Great Wall of China

❓ Who built the Great Wall of China?

Shih Huang-ti was a great Chinese ruler, who was the first to conquer other Chinese leaders and govern an empire. He ordered work to start on the Great Wall in about 220 BC. After he died, he was buried in a huge tomb, with a vast army of more than 6,000 life-sized pottery statues of his warriors and their horses.

Stonehenge builders used horses and carts to shift the stones.

FALSE. The stones were brought to the site and put up using human muscle power.

The Great Wall is visible from space.

TRUE. It's the world's longest structure, at about 6,400 km long.

Which Roman babies were looked after by a wolf?

Romulus, Remus and the wolf

The Romans believed that Rome, their capital city in Italy, was established in 753 BC by a man called Romulus, the son of Mars, the god of war. Roman legends also told how Romulus and his twin brother Remus were stolen from their mother when they were babies, and thrown into the River Tiber. The twins were supposed to have been saved by a wolf, who fed and cared for them as if they were her own cubs.

Murder of Julius Caesar

Julius Caesar

? *Why was Julius Caesar stabbed to death?*

Julius Caesar was a Roman politician who was murdered in 44 BC by fellow politicians – they feared he wanted to overthrow the democratic government and make himself king. The Romans did end up with a kind of king though, because in 27 BC Augustus Caesar became the first Roman emperor.

TRUE OR FALSE?

Julius Caesar invaded Britain.

TRUE. He conquered France and invaded Britain twice.

Julius Caesar built Hadrian's Wall.

FALSE. The Emperor Hadrian started work on a huge stone wall across northern Britain in AD 122.

❓ What did Roman soldiers do with tortoises?

The tortoise was a Roman attack formation. Soldiers made a tough tortoise-shell shape around themselves with their shields, as protection against enemy weapons.

Tortoise

❓ Which weapons did Roman soldiers use?

Roman soldiers fought with spears and swords. Their armour included a helmet, a breastplate and, of course, a shield.

Roman road building

? *What did soldiers do when they weren't fighting?*

It was a tough life in the Roman army. When they weren't fighting battles, soldiers were often hard at work building roads. Engineers used special measuring tools to work out the shortest and most direct route, which is why Roman roads are famous for being straight.

? Did the Romans watch clowns at the Circus?

No, the Circus Maximus was a famous stadium in Rome, where chariot races were held.

Thousands of people went every week to cheer their favourite team, rather like football matches today. Instead of club names, though, the teams had colours – blue, red, green and white.

? *Who gave the thumbs up to gladiators?*

Another favourite day out was a visit to the amphitheatre to watch fighters called gladiators. Usually, pairs of gladiators fought until one of them was defeated and killed. But if the crowd was in a good mood, people would give the thumbs up sign to show they wanted the loser to live.

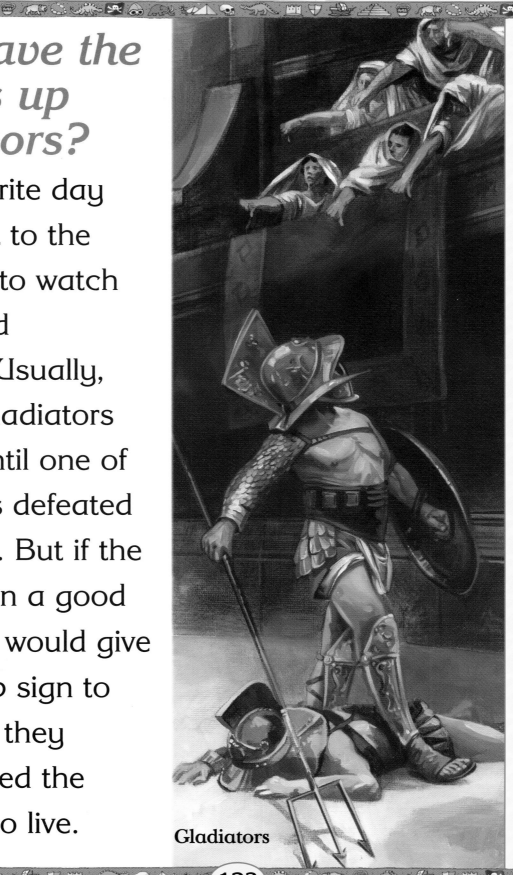

Gladiators

? Why did Romans live in high-rises?

When space got tight in big cities like Rome, landlords built upwards – some blocks of flats were six storeys high. The flats were often badly built, and the ones in Rome were particularly famous for falling down.

Roman buildings

? When did girls get married?

Roman wedding

Many Roman girls were married by their 12th birthday. Girls and boys from wealthy families went to school when they were 7, but girls left at 11 years old, and boys finished some time between their 16th and 18th birthdays.

? *What happened to the Romans?*

At the height of their power, in the AD 100s, the Romans ruled much of Europe and the Middle East, as well as the north coast of Africa. The Empire then began to crumble. It was attacked by tribes from the north and the east, and in AD 476 a Germanic warrior called Odoacer declared himself king of Italy.

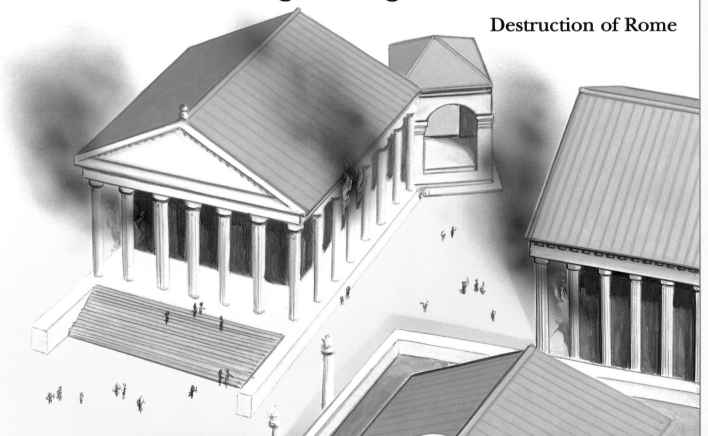

Destruction of Rome

Index